I USED TO HAVE A PLAN

BVT LIFE HAD OTHER IDEAS

ALESSANDRA OLANOW

HARPER DESIGN
An Imprint of HarperCollins Publishers

for coco and mom,
my hearts.

100% VULNERABLE

BE GENTLE
WITH ME.

INTRODUCTION

I NEVER FELT COMFORTABLE WITH CHANGE. EVEN AS A LITTLE GIRL, I CLUNG
TO MY ROUTINES, ALWAYS WANTING TO BE SURE OF WHAT CAME NEXT.
I RESISTED RISK WHOLEHEARTEDLY, SO I GUESS IT'S NOT SURPRISING THAT
MY CHOICES FELL SAFELY WITHIN MY COMFORT ZONE AND MY LIFE
UNFOLDED AS PREDICTABLY AS I COULD PLAN IT.

BUT IT DIDN'T STAY THAT WAY. IN FACT, EVERYTHING FELL APART.
SEEMINGLY OUT OF NOWHERE, AND ALL AT ONCE, I FOUND MYSELF
WITH A BROKEN MARRIAGE, AN EVAPORATING CAREER, AND A DYING MOM.
IT FELT LIKE A HEAVY ROCK HAD DROPPED RIGHT ON TOP OF MY
CHEST AND LEFT ME GASPING FOR AIR.

I TRIED TO IGNORE WHAT WAS HAPPENING AND PRETEND THAT NOTHING WAS
WRONG, BUT THIS WAS IMPOSSIBLE. THEN I BECAME DESPERATE TO FIGURE OUT
HOW TO FIX EVERYTHING, BUT I DIDN'T EVEN KNOW WHERE TO START.

SO I DREW, AND DRAWING BECAME MY COPING MECHANISM. I SKETCHED
THE UPS AND DOWNS OF MY LIFE, WHICH GAVE ME AN ABILITY TO LOOK AT
MY PAIN MORE OBJECTIVELY. AS I CONTINUED TO DRAW MY FEELINGS,
I STARTED TO FIND A SENSE OF SELF AS WELL AS A SENSE OF HUMOR ABOUT
LIFE; WITH TIME, MY RESISTANCE TO CHANGE SOFTENED. I BEGAN TO
EXAMINE MY FEELINGS OF DISCOMFORT, FEELINGS I HADN'T BEEN WILLING
TO LOOK AT BEFORE. IN DOING SO, I DISCOVERED THAT I WAS ABLE TO
HANDLE DIFFICULT EMOTIONS — I DIDN'T NEED TO PUSH THEM AWAY ANYMORE.
BEING OPEN, NO MATTER HOW UNCOMFORTABLE THAT MIGHT BE, HAS
ALLOWED ME TO GROW AND MADE MY LIFE RICHER AND MORE COMPLETE.

I USED TO HAVE A PLAN. NOW I DON'T, NOT REALLY, ANYWAY. MY LIFE
MAY BE MESSIER THAN IT USED TO BE, BUT I HAVE NEVER BEEN CLEARER
AND HAPPIER ABOUT WHO I AM.

THIS BOOK IS A TRIBUTE TO LETTING GO OF MY NEED FOR PREDICTABILITY
AND EMBRACING LIFE, WITH ITS TWISTS AND TURNS.

TO EVERYONE WHO FEELS THEY'VE BEEN TURNED UPSIDE DOWN AND
ARE TRYING TO FIND THE RIGHT WAY UP AGAIN, I HOPE A PAGE OR TWO
FROM MY BOOK OFFERS YOU COMFORT. PLEASE REMEMBER — THIS BEING
HUMAN BUSINESS IS HARD WORK. ♥, ALESSANDRA

part one:
i didn't see that coming.

HELLO, WORLD.

I'LL BE RIGHT BACK.

THIS WAS NOT HOW IT
WAS SUPPOSED TO GO.

I HAD A PLAN.

IT WAS ALL HOW IT
WAS SUPPOSED TO BE.

AND THEN IT WASN'T.

EVERYTHING CAN CHANGE
IN AN INSTANT.

I'M JUST GOING TO LIE
DOWN FOR A LITTLE WHILE.

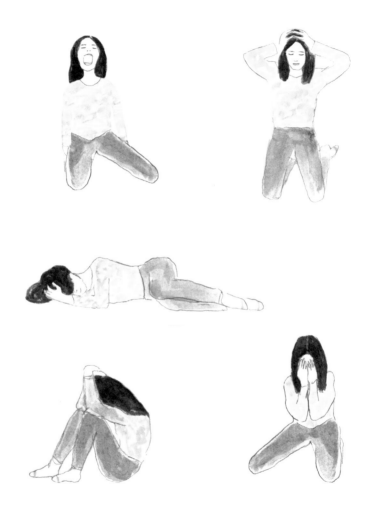

YOU CAN'T SKIP
THIS PART.

SOMETIMES THINGS HAVE TO FALL APART

SO THEY CAN FALL TOGETHER.

Tuesday.

Dear Pain,

Thank you for stopping me dead in my tracks
and showing me what is really important.
It's been educational, but you can go now.

Sincerely,

Me

THE PAINFUL TIMES,
THE ONES WE THINK
WILL BURY US...

ARE OFTEN THE
EXACT ONES THAT
OPEN US UP.

A BROKEN HEART
IS AN OPEN HEART.

part two:
it's okay that you're not okay.

SOME DAYS ARE
HARDER THAN OTHERS.

EXPERIMENTING

AND

FAILING

AN AUTOBIOGRAPHY

BAD IDEAS

			/				/				/				/			
			/				/				/				/			
			/				/				/				/			
			/				/				/				/			
			/				/				/				/			
			/				/				/	

WHAT I THINK

e

WHAT I SAY

I'LL JUST STAY INSIDE.

```
                    kWIKY-FIX
                  OPEN 24 HOURS
                  ANYTOWN,USA


DORITOS NACHO FLAVOR              2.15
CHEESE PUFFS                     2.50
CHEETOS                          2.50
CHEESE POPCORN                   0.99
CHEESE NIPS                      2.59
GOLDFISH                         3.59
HOSTESS CUPCAKES                 2.20
DRAKE'S COFFEE CAKE              3.49
KIT-KAT                          0.87
SUN CHIPS                        3.00
SKITTLES                         3.19
SOUR PATCH KIDS                  2.99
TWIZZLERS                        2.29
HARIBO GUMMI BEARS               2.99
LA CROIX PAMPLEMOUSSE            4.39
LA CROIX PASSIONFRUIT            4.39
LA CROIX MANGO                   4.39
COKE ZERO                        3.79
SCHWEPPES GINGER ALE             3.33
NUTELLA                          2.50
REESE'S PEANUT BUTTER CUPS       0.87
SALTINES                         2.89
STOUFFER'S FRENCH BREAD PIZZA    2.99
BEN & JERRY'S CHUNKY MONKEY      4.89
SNICKERS ICE CREAM BARS          4.99
JELLO                            2.39
ALTOIDS                          1.89
ALKA-SELTZER                     8.42
PEPTO-BISMOL                    10.99
KLEENEX ULTRA-SOFT/JUMBO PACK   22.49


              TOTAL:    $120.94



              THANK YOU!
         SEE YOU NEXT BREAKDOWN!
```

JUST ONE MORE BITE.

TODAY I WILL LIVE IN THE MOMENT
AND THAT MOMENT IS IN BED.

YOU ARE ALLOWED
TO TAKE YOUR TIME.

dear self,

it's okay to check out
for a while, just
remember to check
back in.

love,
me

DON'T MAKE PERMANENT DECISIONS

BASED ON TEMPORARY FEELINGS.

LIKE THE MOON...

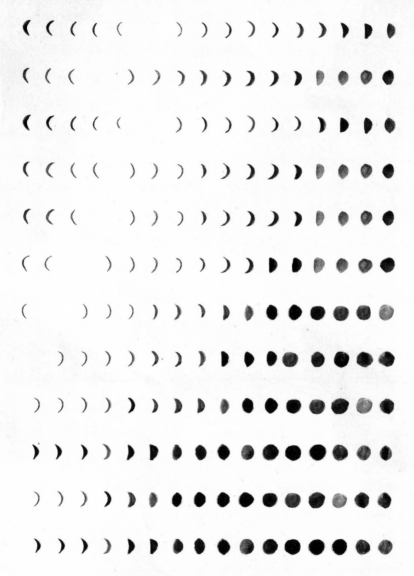

WE GO THROUGH PHASES OF BEING FULL

AND WE GO THROUGH PHASES OF BEING HIDDEN.

•

↖

START WITH
ONE SMALL
POSITIVE THOUGHT

part three:
where'd i go

MAYBE IF I
CHANGE MY HAIR
IT WILL ALL
WORK OUT.

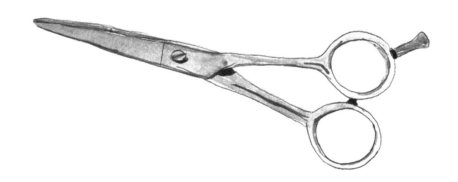

SOME OF OUR GREATEST BATTLES
ARE WITH OURSELVES.

Hello

I THOUGHT I KNEW
WHAT I WAS DOING,
BUT ACTUALLY I DON'T.

YOU (PAUSE) DON'T (PAUSE) HAVE (PAUSE) TO (PAUSE) FIGURE

(PAUSE) IT (PAUSE) ALL (PAUSE) OUT (PAUSE) AT (PAUSE) ONCE.

SOMETIMES IT DOESN'T
HAVE TO MAKE SENSE.

(AND SOMETIMES IT DOESN'T MAKE SENSE.)

SOMETIMES YOU JUST
NEED TO SIT STILL
AND BREATHE.

I KNOW THIS
TOO SHALL PASS.

(BUT IT WOULD BE
HELPFUL TO KNOW WHEN.)

part four:
the only way out is through

AND THIS IS THE PART
WHERE YOU FIND OUT
WHO YOU ARE.

START

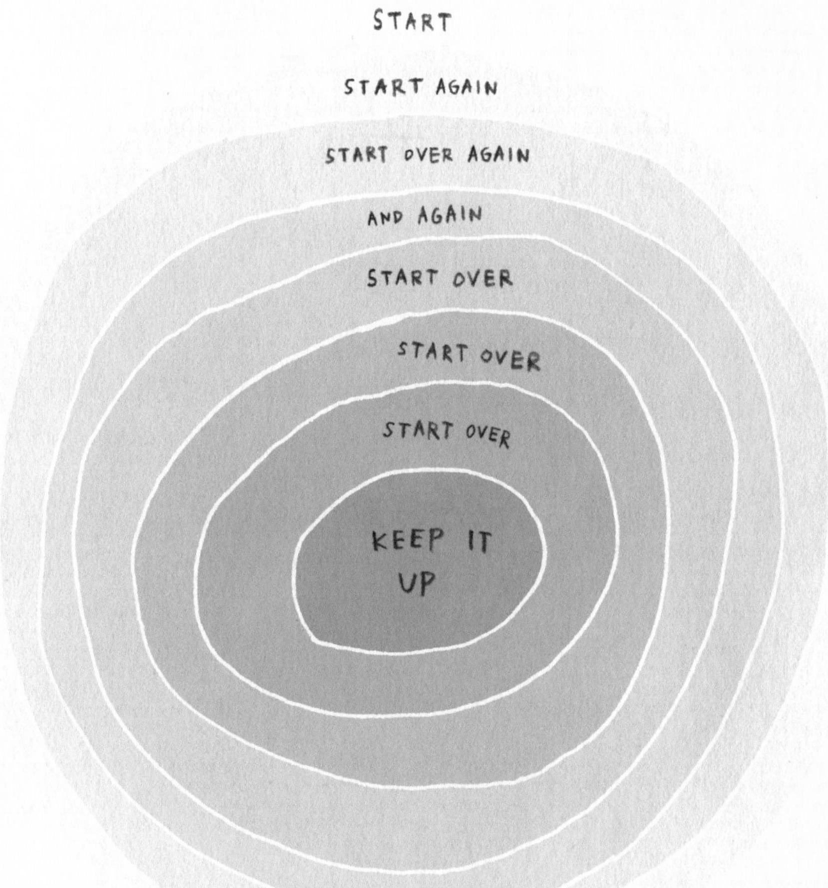

START

START AGAIN

START OVER AGAIN

AND AGAIN

START OVER

START OVER

START OVER

KEEP IT
UP

SURRENDER.

MEMO

TO: SELF

NOTE:

GET OUT OF
YOUR OWN WAY.

(SERIOUSLY, MOVE.)

UNPACK YOUR FEELINGS.

IF IT COMES
LET IT.

IF IT GOES
LET IT.

I HAD TO LET GO
TO REALIZE THERE
WAS NOTHING THERE
TO HOLD ON TO.

HOW TO STOP WORRYING ABOUT WHAT PEOPLE THINK OF YOU

A LIFE'S WORK

GROW THROUGH
WHAT YOU GO THROUGH.

ON THE OTHER SIDE
OF FEAR IS FREEDOM.

INHALE

EXHALE

I'M ~~NOT~~ ENOUGH.

part five:
i like it here, can i stay a while?

me to me.

DEAR SELF,

I'M NOT WHERE
I WANT TO BE,
BUT AT LEAST I'M
NOT WHERE I USED TO BE.

XO,
ME

HOW TO
CHECK YOURSELF

BEFORE YOU
WRECK YOURSELF

(AND OTHER USEFUL STRATEGIES)

SELF

ROLL WITH THE PUNCHES.

BUT DON'T FORGET TO FLY.

REMEMBER, LIFE CHANGES.

X

RESPECT WHERE
YOU ARE.

STAY HOPEFUL. HOPE HELPS.

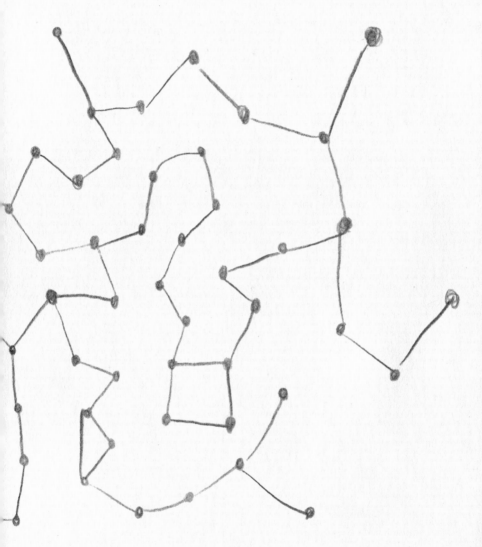

EVENTUALLY EVERYTHING CONNECTS.

I HAVE NO IDEA WHERE I'M GOING,

BUT I'M ON MY WAY.

thank you

delfina balda
margaret brown
heather corbett
betil dagdelen
eleanor forster
cristina garces
daniela jung
tim matusch
andrew olanow
jake ottmann
tiffany pentz
sasha stern
elizabeth sullivan
kate woodrow

and my dad,
warren olanow

First published in 2020 by
Harper Design
An Imprint of HarperCollins Publishers
195 Broadway
New York, NY 10007
Tel: (212) 207-7000
Fax: (855) 746-6023
harperdesign@harpercollins.com
www.hc.com

Distributed throughout the world by
HarperCollins Publishers
195 Broadway
New York, NY 10007

ISBN 978-0-06-297362-7
Library of Congress Control Number: 2020017951

Book design by Alessandra Olanow

Printed in Korea

First Printing, 2020

About the Author

Alessandra Olanow is an illustrator and writer who
lives with her daughter, Coco, in Brooklyn, New York.